You Can
Change the
World

Monika Davies

Publishing Credits

Rachelle Cracchiolo, M.S.Ed., *Publisher*
Conni Medina, M.A.Ed., *Managing Editor*
Nika Fabienke, Ed.D., *Series Developer*
June Kikuchi, *Content Director*
John Leach, *Assistant Editor*
Kevin Pham, *Graphic Designer*

TIME For Kids and the TIME For Kids logo are registered trademarks of TIME Inc. Used under license.

Image Credits: Cover and p.1 Jason Guiterrez/AFP/Getty Images; p.4 Pool-Rpe Nieboer/Katwijk/dpa/picture-alliance/Newscom; p.5 Ariel Skelley Blend Images/Newscom; p.7 Juda Ngwenya/Reuters/Newscom; p.8 KidsRights Foundation; p.9 (top) Siphiwe Sibeko/Reuters/Newscom, (bottom) Rajesh_Jantilal/epa/Newscom; p.10 (Francia) KidsRights Foundation, (Neha) Patrick Van Katwijk/dpa/picture-alliance/Newscom, (Mayra) Robin Utrecht/ANP/Newscom; p.11 (Malala) Andy Rain/EPA/Newscom, (Kehkashan) Jerry Lampen/EPA/Newscom, (Om Prakash) KidsRights Foundation, (Abraham) Bart Maat/EPA/Newscom, (Kesz) Ilvy Njiokiktjien/ANP/Newscom, (Nkosi) Juda Ngwenya/Reuters/Newscom, (Baruani) Phil Nijhuis/Pool/EPA/Newscom, (Chaeli) Robert Vos/EPA/Newscom, (Thandiwe) STR/Reuters/Newscom; p.13 Gary van Wy Photography; p.14 Chaeli Campaign; p.15 Robert Vos/EPA/Newscom; p.16 Jason Guiterrez/AFP/Getty Images; p.19 Ilvy Njiokiktjien/ANP/Newscom; p.20 Suzanne Plunkett/Reuters/Newscom; p.21 Fayaz Aziz/Reuters; p.22 HarperCollins Publishers; p.23 Dennis Van Tine/Geisler-Fotopres/picture alliance/Geisler-Fotop/Newscom; p.24 Balkis Press/ABACA/Newscom; p.25 Robin Utrecht Xinhua News Agency/Newscom; p.26 KidsRights Foundation; p.27 Jerry Lampen/EPA/Newscom; all other images from iStock and/or Shutterstock.

Teacher Created Materials

5301 Oceanus Drive
Huntington Beach, CA 92649-1030
http://www.tcmpub.com

ISBN 978-1-4258-4978-8

© 2018 Teacher Created Materials, Inc.
Printed in China
YiCai.032019.CA201901471

Table of Contents

Courageous Visions

Our world is home to many heroes. These people work hard to help their communities. Some of them are your age! They raise **awareness** for their causes. They make our world more **inclusive**. They protect at-risk kids. And they fight for children's rights.

Every year, one young hero wins the International Children's Peace Prize. A group called KidsRights awards this prize. The award recognizes **courageous** kids. Sometimes, the people who fight hardest for change are the people who need it most.

The world faces many serious problems. These kids are finding ways to solve them. Let's discover how they are making a difference in our world!

Say Hello to Neha

Neha Gupta (NEY-hah GOOP-tuh) won the Children's Peace Prize in 2014. She founded Empower Orphans. It is a charity that provides medical care, food, and clothing to orphans. She came up with the idea when she was only nine years old!

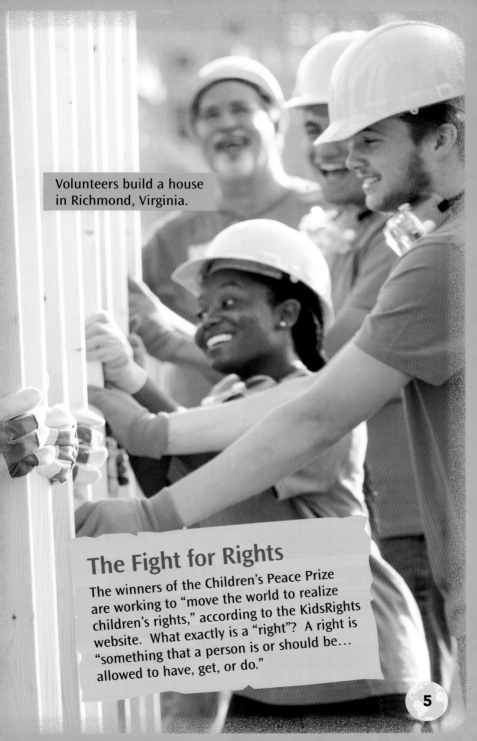

Volunteers build a house in Richmond, Virginia.

The Fight for Rights

The winners of the Children's Peace Prize are working to "move the world to realize children's rights," according to the KidsRights website. What exactly is a "right"? A right is "something that a person is or should be... allowed to have, get, or do."

Nkosi Johnson

In July 2000, a young boy stood on a stage in front of 10,000 people. He wore a dark blue suit. His pants were baggy. He wore sneakers.

"Hi, my name is Nkosi (nuh-KOH-see) Johnson," he said. "I am 11 years old, and I have full-blown AIDS."

Nkosi spoke at the International AIDS Conference in South Africa. Nkosi's mother was HIV-positive. He had been born infected. This meant he was already sick and might not live long. At the time, many infected South African children died before they turned two. Nkosi hoped to help change this.

What Are HIV and AIDS?

HIV is a virus that hurts the immune system. The immune system keeps you from getting sick. People get AIDS when the HIV virus has taken over. But HIV-positive people can live long lives with proper treatment.

HIV virus

"We Are All Human Beings"

Nkosi's speech at the International AIDS Conference changed lives. This is because he spoke from the heart. He said, "You can't get AIDS if you touch, hug, kiss, hold hands with someone who is infected." His message was powerful: "Don't be afraid of us—we are all the same."

Nkosi's foster mom is Gail Johnson. In 1997, she tried to enroll him in school. But school officials said no. They thought that having an HIV-positive student in the school would be unsafe. Many people were afraid of AIDS. Fear made them **exclude** those who were infected.

Gail was upset. She went to the newspapers. Word spread about the unfair situation. The pressure from the **media** made the school change its decision. Nkosi was able to go to school.

Nkosi began to fight for awareness. He wanted to erase the **stigma** of having AIDS. His speech in 2000 was powerful. It made people stop and listen. "Care for us and accept us," Nkosi said in his speech. He taught the world to treat HIV-positive people with respect. Sadly, Nkosi passed away when he was only 12 years old. He was the first winner of the Children's Peace Prize.

A "Nkosi"

A Nkosi statue is given to each Children's Peace Prize winner. It shows how a kid can "move" the world. KidsRights also gives prize money to the winner's cause.

Nkosi's Haven

Nkosi was separated from his mother as a young boy. His dream was to offer a safe home to HIV-positive mothers and their kids. Nkosi's Haven brings his dream to life. It is a care center in South Africa that helps those in need.

International Inspirations

Francia Simon
Dominican Republic

Neha Gupta
United States

International Children's Peace Prize winners are making differences all around the globe! Check out which countries they call home.

Mayra Avellar Neves
Brazil

Malala Yousafzai
United Kingdom
(originally from Pakistan)

Kehkashan Basu
United Arab Emirates

Om Prakash Gurjar
India

Kesz Valdez
Philippines

Abraham M. Keita
Liberia

Nkosi Johnson
South Africa

Baruani Ndume
Tanzania

Michaela "Chaeli" Mycroft
South Africa

Thandiwe Chama
Zambia

Chaeli Mycroft

On September 3, 2015, Michaela "Chaeli" Mycroft (KAY-lee MY-krahft) looked out from the top of Mount Kilimanjaro (kih-lih-muhn-JAH-roh). It is Africa's highest mountain. Reaching this mountain's peak is a tough journey for anyone. But Chaeli's climb was special. She had just become the first female **quadriplegic** (kwah-druh-PLEE-jihk) to reach the mountain's summit.

Mount Kilimanjaro

She's a Marathoner

In May 2016, Chaeli was one of the first wheelchair athletes to finish the Comrades Marathon. This is a hard race. It stretches 55 miles (89 kilometers). She and her two running partners formed Team Beastie.

She's a Dancer

Chaeli is a wheelchair dancer. She has been dancing like this since she was 11. Her longtime partner is Damian. Together, they often dance in big competitions.

Chaeli is from South Africa. She was born with cerebral palsy. Her condition has caused her to only be able to move certain parts of her body. She uses a wheelchair to get around.

"I have an **uncooperative** body," she says. "The messages don't get where they need to get." But that has never stopped her. Her goal is to inspire. She works to make the world more inclusive.

At age nine, Chaeli wanted to be more independent. A motorized wheelchair could help her move around on her own. But it was very expensive. Chaeli and her friends raised money for the wheelchair. It took them only seven weeks! With her new wheelchair, Chaeli felt a new sense of freedom.

Chaeli wanted all kids to feel this freedom. She decided to launch the Chaeli Campaign. It helps kids in South Africa. Its purpose is to "**mobilize** the minds and bodies of children with disabilities."

Chaeli still fights for awareness. She reminds people, "It's empowering to have a wheelchair. It's not a negative thing."

Campaign Goals

The Chaeli Campaign helps in many ways. It offers free physical therapy. It gives kids new gear. The campaign works to create inclusive classrooms.

2011 Winner

In 2011, Chaeli won the Children's Peace Prize for her work as an ability **activist**. In her speech, she said, "Hope is what keeps us going. It's what keeps us striving for the lives we deserve."

Kesz Valdez

In 2005, Kesz (KEHS) Valdez turned seven years old. For his birthday, he asked for something unusual—flip-flops to give to street children. Not too long before, Kesz had been living on the streets.

Kesz grew up in Cavite (kuh-VEE-tey) City in the Philippines. His parents treated him badly. He ran away from home. Faced with no food or place to sleep, Kesz began living in a garbage dump.

Then, **tragedy** struck. Kesz fell into a pile of burning tires and was badly hurt. A kind social worker treated Kesz's wounds. He gave Kesz a new home. He became his guardian.

Young and Homeless

The United Nations reports that up to 150 million children in the world are homeless. We need a solution. Kesz and other children are finding ways to help.

Kesz Valdez

STOP! THINK...

Kesz wants to end violence against children. Here are seven *interlinked* strategies to help. A strategy is a "careful plan or method for achieving a goal."

> What do you think the word *interlinked* means?
> What do you think *norms and values* mean?
> How do you think these strategies will help end violence against children?

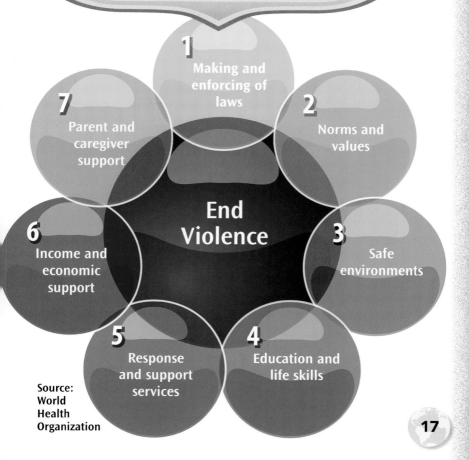

1 Making and enforcing of laws

2 Norms and values

3 Safe environments

4 Education and life skills

5 Response and support services

6 Income and economic support

7 Parent and caregiver support

End Violence

Source: World Health Organization

Because of one man's kindness, Kesz's life changed completely. But Kesz did not forget the street children who had lived beside him. Kesz decided to help them.

Starting on his seventh birthday, he began giving gifts to homeless children. He called them his Gifts of Hope. First, he gave children flip-flops so they would not cut their feet. But Kesz wanted to do more. He began teaching street children how to care for themselves. He showed them how to brush their teeth and treat their wounds. To continue his work, he started an organization called Championing Community Children.

"We are all heroes, no matter how old we are," Kesz said. "We can all move the world."

Missing Out on School

As of 2013, 1 out of every 10 kids in the Philippines did not go to school. That is over four million kids. There were many reasons for them not being in school. Some got married when they were young. Others could not go to school because their families did not have enough money.

Philippines

2012 Winner

Kesz was the 2012 winner of the Peace Prize. His message gives hope to all kids. "Our health is our wealth!" He said, "Being healthy will enable you to play, to think clearly, to get up and go to school, and love the people around you in so many ways."

19

Malala Yousafzai

Every year, a person or group wins the Nobel Peace Prize. The winners have made a big difference in the world. It is a big honor.

In 2014, the prize was awarded to a 17-year-old girl. She was the youngest winner ever. Before her, the youngest winner had been 32 years old.

Her name is Malala Yousafzai (mah-LAH-lah yoo-sahf-ZAY). She is fighting for every child's right to an education. When she accepted the award, people listened to her wise words.

"This award is not just for me," she said. "I am not a lone voice, I am many. I am those 66 million girls who are **deprived** of education."

A Warrior's Name

Malala is named after Malalai of Maiwand. She was a fierce folk hero. In 1880, she raised a banner while her country, Afghanistan, fought the British. Her cry rallied her country's troops to win the battle.

THINK LINK

The Right to an Education

Malala says, "In some parts of the world, students are going to school every day. It's their normal life. But in other parts of the world, we are starving for education…it's like a precious gift. It's like a diamond." Think about the questions below as you read this chapter:

❯ Why do you think going to school is important for all children?

❯ What skills do you learn in school?

❯ Should every person be able to go to high school? Why or why not?

Malala grew up in Pakistan. She lived in the Swat Valley. In 2009, the Taliban gained control of the area where she lived. The Taliban is a dangerous group. It believes that girls should not go to school.

When she was 11 years old, Malala began writing a blog for the BBC, a British news service. She talked about what her life was like. Her words painted a life of fear caused by the Taliban. Many people read her words. Her blog was popular. She first wrote **anonymously**. But she was later revealed as the author.

On October 9, 2012, the Taliban tried to silence Malala. That day, she was on her way to school on a bus. Two men stopped the bus. Then, they shot her in the head. But she survived.

Malala's Bookshelf

As a young child, Malala had only eight books on her bookshelf! Now, she has many more. She believes every girl should read *The Breadwinner* by Deborah Ellis. She says that the best book she has ever read is Paulo Coelho's *The Alchemist*.

Like Father, Like Daughter

Malala is very close to her family, but she has a special bond with her father, Ziauddin (zee-ow-DEEN). He is often asked how he helped Malala become "bold and courageous." He replies, "Don't ask me what I did. Ask me what I did not do. I did not clip her wings, and that's all."

I Am Malala

Would you like to know more about Malala? Her **memoir**, *I Am Malala*, tells her story. The book begins with her childhood in Pakistan. It continues on to her role as an activist.

Malala would not let the Taliban defeat her. She was rushed into surgery. She survived and continues to fight for education for all children.

"I don't want to be remembered as the girl who was shot," she said. "I want to be remembered as the girl who stood up."

Since then, she has established the Malala Fund. It seeks to **empower** girls "to unlock their potential and to demand change." She has been recognized worldwide for her bravery.

Malala continues to be an **advocate** for change. Her words remind people that "One child, one teacher, one book, and one pen can change the world."

2013 Winner

In 2013, Malala won the Children's Peace Prize. In her speech, she said, "I want to live in a world where education is taken for granted in every corner of the globe." She has a vision of a world where no child misses out on the chance to learn.

Inspiring Futures

We are all global citizens. We can all help our world become a brighter place.

Each Children's Peace Prize winner is a strong advocate for his or her cause. These children are helping to shape our world. You can too! People everywhere face daily struggles. Some do not have enough food to eat. Others do not have access to education. No matter what the need, it is important for us to find ways to help one another.

Think of your community. How can you help make your hometown a better place? Remember, change can come from small actions. Anyone can make a difference. But bigger changes happen when we work together.

Fighting for the Planet

Kehkashan Basu (KEH-kuh-shah baw-SOO), from the United Arab Emirates (EHM-uhr-ihts), wants you to act! The 2016 Children's Peace Prize winner fights to protect the environment. She started Green Hope to spread her mission. She helps get young people involved in cleanups and tree planting.

Glossary

activist—a person who uses or supports strong actions to help make changes

advocate—a person who argues for or supports a cause or policy

anonymously—not named or identified

awareness—knowledge of a situation or fact

courageous—very brave

deprived—not having what is needed for a good or healthy life

empower—to give power to (someone)

exclude—to prevent someone from doing something or being part of a group

inclusive—not limited to certain people

media—radio stations, newspapers, and television stations that give information to the public

memoir—a book about someone's life

mobilize—to make ready for action

quadriplegic—a person who is permanently unable to move or feel both arms and both legs because of injury or illness

stigma—a set of negative and often unfair beliefs that a society or group of people have about something

tragedy—a very sad or upsetting event

uncooperative—not willing to do what someone wants or asks for

Index

Check It Out!

Books

Ikink, Inge. 2014. *Changemakers: 10 International Children's Peace Prize Winners Tell Their Remarkable Stories*. CreateSpace Independent Publishing Platform.

Yousafzai, Malala. 2016. *I Am Malala: How One Girl Stood Up for Education and Changed the World* (Young Readers Edition). Little, Brown Books for Young Readers.

Video

TED Talks. *Talks by Brilliant Kids and Teens.* TED.com. www.ted.com/playlists/129/ted _under_20.

Websites

KidsRights. *The International Children's Peace Prize*. www.childrenspeaceprize.org.

KidsRights. *The KidsRights Youngsters.* www.kidsrightsyoungsters.org.

Try It!

Your class can make the world a brighter place! Discuss with your classmates how you can help.

❯ What are some challenges facing young people in your community? Come up with at least three.

❯ Make a list of ways you can address each challenge.

❯ As a group, select one challenge. Research local charities in your area. Do any of them do work that fits with your ideas? If there is no charity or group, what else can you do to make a difference? Make a plan and follow through.

Challenges	How We Can Help
❶	❶
❷	❷
❸	❸

About the Author

Monika Davies is a Canadian writer. She loves learning about children who help their communities. They inspire her to take action! She believes kindness never goes out of style. And she feels people make a difference by working from the heart. Monika also loves to travel! She has been to 38 countries around the world.